Less Time

a Blessing

Pets Are a Blessing

written by
Victoria Ryan

illustrated by
R.W. Alley

ABBEY PRESS

Publications
St. Meinrad, IN 47577

Text © 2014 by Victoria Ryan
Illustrations © 2014 by Saint Meinrad Archabbey
Published by Abbey Press Publications
St. Meinrad, Indiana 47577

Library of Congress Control Number
2014936007

ISBN 978-0-87029-564-5

Printed in the United States of America.

Foreword

Pets are a blessing—in every sense of the word. Beyond the joy of their whimsical personalities and zany antics, they infuse holiness into our lives. They don't just love us; they teach us we are lovable. They aren't just adorable; they prove that all of God's creatures have value. They don't just walk our earthly journey with us; they share our experience through loyal companionship, fierce protection, and unfailing concern.

Pets are a blessing. They sense medical conditions machines can't detect. They uncover criminal activity and provide rehabilitation services. They perform acts of heroic bravery humans cannot, and they do so willingly for owner or stranger. Like ambassadors from heaven, pets are a glimpse of our Creator's steadfast, merciful, and jubilant love.

Pets are a blessing and this book celebrates their gifts, both the simple and the profound. If these affirmations bring a smile of recognition, a seed of new thought, or a renewed awe of God's wisdom in creation, then your pet has blessed you again.

1.

Pets are a blessing. They love us, teach us, and make us laugh.

2.

Pets are blind to age, weight, education, and past sins. They only see a person worthy of love.

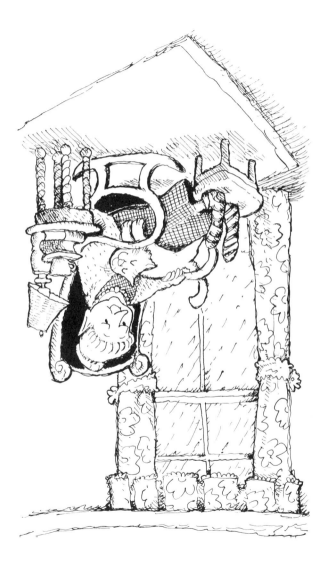

3.

Not all pets are dogs and cats.
Birds, turtles, gerbils, fish—
any animal that trusts you
enough to care for them is
a pet.

4.

A pet's love has no strings attached. A pet hopes for love, but does not demand it.

5.

Pets tolerate sports jerseys, Halloween costumes, and jingle bell hats for your sake, not theirs. They do whatever it takes to please you.

6.

What is true family, if not
a kitten asleep in your slipper
or a dog awaiting your return
at the door?

7.

Few expressions of compassion are more genuine than a dog who digs up his bone and lays it on the lap of his grieving owner.

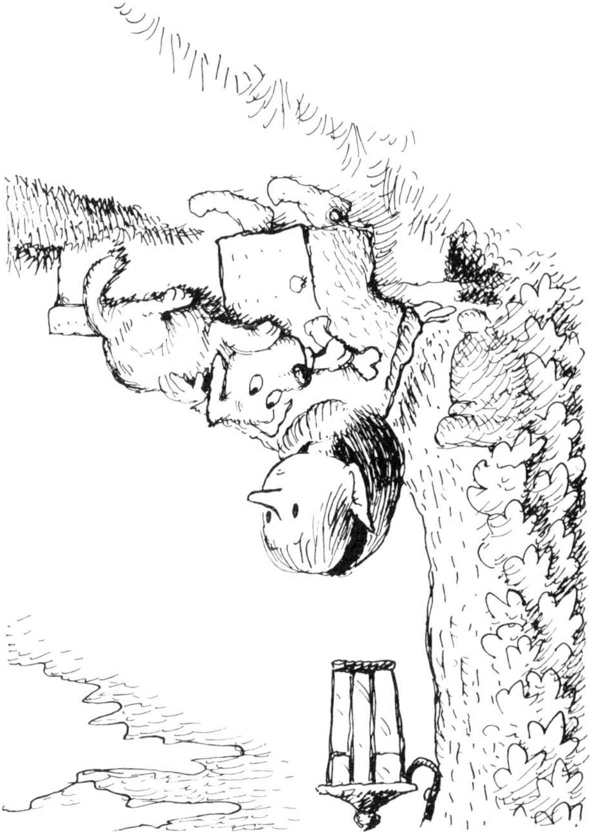

8.

We look to friends for
company; to pets for
solitude.

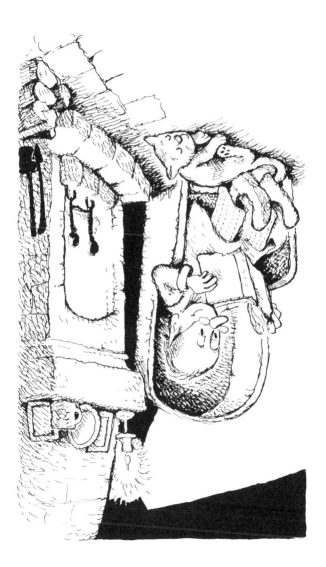

9.

When a pet keeps vigil by your sickbed, it is saying, "You matter to me."

10.

Your relationship with your pet is one of the longest of your life, sometimes outlasting marriage and other friendships.

11.

From cat eyes that glow like coals in the night, to horse eyes so large they mirror your reflection, the physical beauty of pets bring awe to your world.

12.

Owning a pet teaches us
to love those smaller and
weaker than ourselves.

13.

A pet is a velvet splinter that cracks open a hardened heart. Someone who cares for their pet is on the road to caring for their neighbor.

fancy
bunny
Chow

14.

A pet is like a blanket made of silk ribbons, ready to comfort and brighten your soul. Your pet will never ridicule, abandon, or stop loving you.

15.

You can tell your pet *anything*.
Your pet will never divulge
your secrets.

16.

You don't realize how uniquely precious you are until you see yourself through the eyes of your pet.

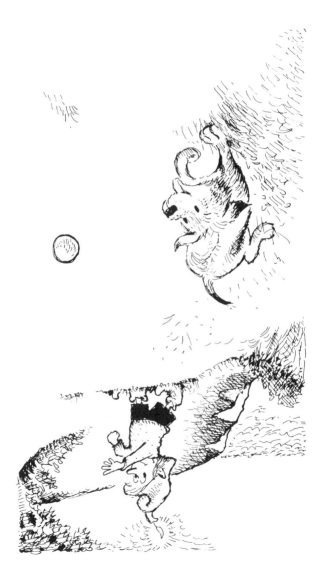

17.

Nature tranquilizes with gurgling brooks, giggling children, and the soft *pit pat, pit pat, pit pat* of paws along the floor.

18.

Pets heal us. Stroking a cat or watching a fish decreases blood pressure, increases sleep, and cuts in half the amount of pain medication needed after surgery.

19.

Search dogs are the Sherlock Holmes of canines. They can pick up the faintest scents, smell insects underground, and locate a single poisonous plant in an acre of crops.

20.

Guide dogs are eyes for the blind, ears for the deaf, and balance for those with artificial limbs. They are the puzzle piece that completes a picture of independence.

21.

Pet dogs are the brave little soldiers of your home, ready to defend you with all their might. Cats are the silent sentinel—unassuming, secretive, and lethal when need be.

22.

Whether from paw prints on your car hood or bones buried in your laundry, pets make you smile when you least expect it.

23.

There are few troubles that aren't diminished by the sight of a dog sticking its head out the window of a passing car.

24.

Pets can sometimes remind
us that we take life too
seriously.

25.

It's difficult to project authority when your commands begin with "Fluffy," "Bubbles," or "Lamb Chop."

26.

Take it from a cat: when one life ends, another one begins.

27.

It's amazing how intelligent animal greeting cards sound once you own a pet. Celebrate the humor and joy pets provide.

28.

It may be true, as
Carl Sandburg said, that
fog comes in on little
cats' feet. But it's the cat
pouncing on your chest
at daybreak that takes your
breath away.

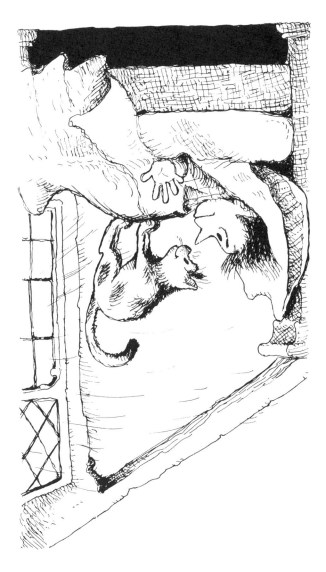

29.

Nothing solves the mystery of a missing cookie more definitively than crumb-covered whiskers.

30.

If it could rain pet cats and pet dogs all over the world, there would be fewer people hungry for love and protection.

31.

World peace summits should never convene without first watching a group of puppies, kittens, and children wrestling with glee in the park.

32.

For a pet, it is never about "things," it is always about your love.

33.

Pets remind us to be true to ourselves. After all, it is easier to believe that the lion will lay down with the lamb than it is to fathom the dog laying down with the squirrels.

34.

There are three things you will never forget: your 16th birthday, your high school graduation, and the day you welcomed your pet into your home.

35.

You know you have the right
pet when you believe that no
one ever has or ever will
cherish their pet as much
as you cherish yours.

36.

The greatest gift of a pet is
knowing—forever—that
you are loved.

Victoria Ryan writes for children and adults. She has published articles and essays in national markets and was a finalist in the 2012 Tuscany Prize for Catholic Fiction. Her second book, *When Your Pet Dies* (Abbey Press) is dedicated to her first pet, a yellow lab. She and her husband are now the proud owners of Bartholomew Francis Ryan the First, a border collie-lab they adopted from a rescue animal shelter.

Illustrator for the Abbey Press Elf-help Books, **R.W. Alley** also illustrates and writes children's books. He lives in Barrington, Rhode Island, with his wife, daughter, and son. See a wide variety of his works at: www.rwalley.com.

The Story of the Abbey Press Elves

The engaging figures that populate the Abbey Press "elf-help" line of publications and products first appeared in 1987 on the pages of a small self-help book called *Be-good-to-yourself Therapy*. Shaped by the publishing staff's vision and defined in R.W. Alley's inventive illustrations, they lived out author Cherry Hartman's gentle, self-nurturing advice with charm, poignancy, and humor.

Reader response was so enthusiastic that more Elf-help Books were soon under way, a still-growing series.

The especially endearing character featured in the early books—sporting a cap with a mood-changing candle in its peak—has since been joined by a spirited female elf with flowers in her hair.

These two exuberant, sensitive, resourceful, kindhearted, lovable sprites, along with their lively elfin community, reveal what's truly important as they offer messages of joy and wonder, playfulness and co-creation, wholeness and serenity, the miracle of life and the mystery of God's love.

With wisdom and whimsy, they demonstrate the elf-help way to a rich and fulfilling life.

Elf-help Books

...adding "a little character" and a lot
of help to self-help reading!

Overcoming-jealousy-and-envy Therapy	#20827
Grieving With a Grateful Heart	#20824
Elf-help for Living With Joy	#20498
Empty Nest Therapy	#20489
Pets Are a Blessing	#20480
You Are an Amazing Woman	#20464
Scripture's Way to Live Each Day	#20444
When Your Parent Dies	#20369
On the Anniversary of Your Loss	#20363
Elf-help for Coping with Cancer	#20359
Believe-in-yourself Therapy	#20351
Grieving at Christmastime	#20052
Grief Therapy	#20178
Healing Thoughts for Troubled Hearts	#20058
Take Charge of Your Eating	#20064

Elf-help for Coping With Pain #20074

Elf-help for Dealing with Difficult People #20076

Loneliness Therapy #20078

'Tis a Blessing to Be Irish #20088

Getting Older, Growing Wiser #20089

Worry Therapy #20093

Trust-in-God Therapy #20119

Elf-help for Overcoming Depression #20134

New Baby Therapy #20140

Teacher Therapy #20145

Stress Therapy #20153

Get Well Therapy #20157

Anger Therapy #20127

Caregiver Therapy #20164

Self-esteem Therapy #20165

Peace Therapy #20176

Friendship Therapy #20174

Christmas Therapy (color edition) $5.95 #20175

Happy Birthday Therapy	#20181
Forgiveness Therapy	#20184
Keep-life-simple Therapy	#20185
Acceptance Therapy	#20190
Keeping-up-your-spirits Therapy	#20195
Slow-down Therapy	#20203
One-day-at-a-time Therapy	#20204
Prayer Therapy	#20206
Be-good-to-your-marriage Therapy	#20205
Be-good-to-yourself Therapy	#20255

Available at your favorite gift shop or bookstore—
or directly from Abbey Press Publications,
St. Meinrad, IN 47577.
Call 1-800-325-2511.
www.abbeypresspublications.com